SCREW STUDENT LOANS

"How to Destroy Student Loans, Slap
Sallie Mae around and Organize your
Life to pay off your Debt"

Brian A. Cliette

Screw Student Loans

"How to Destroy Student Loans, Slap Sallie Mae around and
Organize your Life to pay off your Debt"

©2015, Brian A. Cliette All rights reserved.

BULLCITY
PUBLISHING

This eBook and supplementary material was created to provide specific information regarding the subject matter covered. Every attempt has been made to verify the information provided in this material however neither the author nor the publisher are responsible for any errors, omissions, or incorrect interpretations of the subject matter.

Information contained within this material is subject to local, state, federal and international laws. The reader is advised to consult with a licensed professional for legal, financial and other professional services.

The reader of this material assumes responsibility for the use of this information. Adherence to all applicable laws and regulations governing professional licensing, business practices, advertising and all other aspects of doing business in the United States or any other jurisdiction is the sole responsibility of the reader.

The author and publisher assume no responsibility or liability whatsoever for the use or misuse of the information contained within these materials.

From the Desk James Moore Editor of Bull City Publishing:

Dear Friend,

If at Any point while you're reading this book you have any questions, please don't hesitate to contact us. You can best reach us at Twitter (@bullcitypub), or on our Facebook Fan Page

Even if you don't have any questions, We'd love for you to come by and say hello! If you want to reach us in a private you can email us at info@bullcitypublishing.com or on our blog Bullcitypublishing.com/blog

Warmest Regards,

James Moore

EDITOR & CHIEF ,BULL CITY PUBLISHING, LLC

Do you Love Reading? Do you Want a Ton of FREE Kindle Books? Join our Mailing list by Emailing us at freebooks@bullcitypublishing.com

CONTENTS

CHAPTER 1:

INTRODUCTION

A recent statistics has shown that the problem of student loans has shown a steep increase of around 1000% in the last 10 years. Applying for a student loan is an inevitable step while getting admission to the university or any establishment offering higher education owing to the fact that higher education is way too expensive for any average citizen to be able to afford. Unless you come from an excessively affluent background, you are sure to get yourself a loan much before you get the degree.

It has also been observed that the fee hike for higher education establishments has been as high as 27% in the last 5 years, which has worsened the situation even more. The gravity of the issue can be well understood by looking at the case of a Chilean activist who stole and burnt his $500 million loan papers. He was compelled to act in this manner because the university that he was enrolled to was being shut down for the financial irregularities in their system. He feared transfer of this loan to an establishment that would take actions like eviction and foreclosures, in addition to several other severe calls that universities usually take.

Time and again, there have been several movements that have demanded action from the Government on finding a viable solution to this seemingly ever-growing issue. A popular initiative taken in this direction is the 'Pay As You Make' initiative, which demands you to align payments with increase in income. In addition to limiting interest amounts, this initiative prevents people from indulging into institutional practices that increase debt to unimaginable levels. However, the recommendations of this initiative have been found to be excessively inadequate.

The biggest problem with student loans is that students take up the loan with the hope that they will make repayments in favor of this loan from the income that they generate after they get a job. However, if the market is not in a good position, this job may not even come to them. As a result, the income will not be there and loan repayment will become difficult.

With this said, it is equally important to mention that there are several methods and ways that can be followed to manage student loans easily. All that most of these methods require is persistence and discipline. Besides this, you may also decide to look into forgiveness plans to get rid of your loans. Most of these plans have been created to reduce the pressure on students. So, they reduce the repayment amount by as much as 50% to make repayment easier.

Keeping in mind the fact that these loans are taken by students who begin to repay them only a little time after they have finished college. Therefore, expecting them to have the understanding and presence of mind to explore all the options and make a strategic plan to put off the loans on them, can be way to much to ask for from a 22-year old. This is the reason why professional advice must be taken in this regard to make the individual aware about some of the repay options that people may not have any idea about.

One of the biggest factors that come into play is stress. When you delay repayment to a point that repayment amount rises to unimaginable levels, you will inevitably be stressed. Therefore, if you have a student loan, do not ignore it. You can't even imagine the consequences you may have to face because of this. You may not be able to get a credit card or loan for business for the rest of your life. So, take your loans seriously enough to repay them on time and not seriously enough to take undue stress for it.

CHAPTER 2:

UNDERSTANDING STUDENT LOAN BASICS

For years, people have been complaining about the fact that higher education is getting expensive by the day. This has made higher education available and accessible only to the people who can afford it. It is usually too expensive for average people to afford the expenses related to classes, tuitions and basic facilities that are required for attending university or college. To help such parents and students, Governments of several countries decided to come with a financial support plan, which are now popularly known as student loans.

How are student loans different from other loans?

The four fundamental differences between student loans and general loans are:

- Student loans involve much lower rates of interest

- The repayment period for student loans are usually higher

- The repayment period does not start while the student is studying and starts only after the student gets a job or a stipulated period of time post completion of course has passed, whichever is earlier.

- There are stricter lows for renegotiation and bankruptcy cover for student loans as opposed to general loans.

Types of Student Loans

Student loans can be of two types. The first of these two types is a state-sanctioned loan, which is usually government-sponsored and offered via a non-profit government establishment. In addition, these loans are mostly a part of the whole student package, which may also include grants, scholarships and work while you study opportunities.

Most student loans fall under this category. The biggest advantage that this type of loans offer is that the student is not expected to pay interest for the time when he or she was still studying at the university or college. Students who get this loan either get the same as part of a scholarship offered by the government or a loan from a private lender upon the guarantee given by the government.

Although, this type of student loans has several benefits, it has faced immense criticism in the past for giving the lenders a great opportunity to make excessive profits while the students weren't getting any significant benefits from the same. This is perhaps the reason why, today, you will find it difficult to locate any government-guaranteed loan being offered. However, the only student loans of such type that are still available are ones that are given to special cases like students with medical impairments.

This brings us to the other type of student loans. This type of student loans is a loan that is given out to students by financial organizations or lender in much the same manner as any other loan. Several legislations cover the repayment of these loans. However, with this said, it is vital to mention here that this type of a student loan proves more expensive to a student as compared to the first type of student loans.

Regardless of what the origin of the student loan is, government or private organization, student loans cannot be forgiven. However, if the repayment of the loan is causing intolerable hardship for the student or anyone who is depend on him or her. In order to sort this issue out, the repayment of student loans is scheduled on the basis of the income of the student.

Eligibility Requirements For Student Loans

Different organizations and establishments have different eligibility requirements, which the student needs to fulfill if he or she wishes to get a loan. If a student has criminal history or has been involved in substance abuse in the past, then the student's loan application is directly rejected. For others, the loan sanction largely depends on the total family income of the student.

Moreover, the amount of loan that a student can apply for is also limited. The two factors that determine the amount of loan that can be sanctioned include the student's educational level (graduate or post-graduate) and how dependent or independent the student is.

If a student has applied for a loan from a private organization, then there may be several other requirements that the student shall be required to fulfill. The first and foremost requirement is a guarantor. A student's guarantor can be his or her parent, relative or guardian. It has been observed in the recent past that students apply for loans from private organization only after they have used up their credit limit for government student loans.

Unlike other loans, the repayment tenure for a student loan does not begin as soon as the loan is sanctioned and accepted by the borrower. In fact, in this case, the repayment period doesn't start during the time of the student's education. If the student fails to get a job immediately, the repayment tenure starts after more than 6 months to 1 year from the date when the student's course finishes or the student leaves education because of expulsion of dropping out.

Typically, the agreement has all the details regarding the repayment schedule and time. However, if the student fails to repay from the stipulated date and finish the loan within the specified time, the agreement also allows the borrower to ask the lender for an extension on loan tenure.

While student loans give students the opportunity to study further despite being short of finances, it also burdens them with loan repayment, putting immense pressure on them, particularly if they have dependents on them. This is the reason why the concept of helping out students who wish to study further, but do not have the financial support required via student loans has been gravely criticized.

Students who take up these loans also have been observed to feel burdened and dissatisfied by the poor implementation of the intent. In fact, some students have gone to the extent of saying that they feel that the loan providers are victimizing them. On the other hand, scholars and academicians feel that the idea of giving out loans to the needy was based on the intent to help the society. Therefore, they should either be given out on a 'cost to cost' basis or below cost.

Moreover, they argue that the benefits of educating the youth will lower costs and generate revenues, which clearly outweigh the risks involved in giving the loan. So, even if a student is unable to repay the loan, the way he or she uses his gained knowledge in the society will be worth much more than the cost of the loan.

In a recent finding, it was observed that educational institutions were using student loans as a tool to make money. They recommended a certain lender for getting student loan and received a commission for the same from the lender. Irrespective of the malpractices that exist in the market, the truth of the matter is that students who cannot afford the high costs of education will need to take student loans. However, students must never take the pressure on them. You have a lot of options available and in-hand for you. The most prominent of the available options is repayment plan adjustment, which shall allow you to repay the loan as per your financial condition.

CHAPTER 3:

GETTING TO KNOW
WHAT YOUR STUDENT LOAN INCLUDES

On an average, it has been seen that a student studying at a government university graduates with a loan of around $25,000 on him or her. However, if you are studying in a private university, you can safely escalate this figure to a six-digit value. Now, if you look at the salaries that average graduates receive, you will realize that the average salary is around $40,000. The numbers speak for themselves that repayment of the loan in the mentioned salary is an uphill task, for sure.

If you leave things as they are, you will undoubtedly end up in the case that we just mentioned. Fortunately, there are ways and means that can help you manage your debt rather well. However, the first step towards effective debt management is to know the following things about your loan.

Loan Specifics And Grace Period

Some basic things about your loan that you must always have on your fingertips include:

- Who is the lender?

- How much money that you presently owe?

- What are the different loans that you have running on your name?

- What is the repayment status and details of each of your loans?

- What is the grace period for your loan? Grace period can simply be described as the time for which the lender will wait until repayment begins. Remember that grace period differs from one loan to the next. Therefore, be sure to check and keep track of your grace period.

These are some things that you must know even if you have entrusted the responsibility of managing your finances to someone else in the family for the simple reason that if something goes wrong, you are the one who will be find accountable and questioned.

Never Ignore Your Loans

As we mentioned previously, the repayment for student loans is secured by a strict legislation. So, if you take the loan and just forget about it, the legal system of the country will hunt you down and remind you of the every single penny that you owe. Moreover, even if you manage to escape the legislative proceedings, you will never be able to take a loan on your name. In fact, you won't be able to get even a credit card in your name.

While the legislation protects the lender to ensure that the borrower returns the money borrowed, it also issues some rights to the borrower as far as loan repayment is concerned. Here are the options and rights that you possess.

Knowing Your Options

If you have landed up into financial trouble and repayment of loan is looking like a tough call to you, then before you start panicking, remember that you still have some options with you. You can avail these options to delay the repayment of loans. You must go through the laws specific to your loan and negotiate with your lender, communicating your situation and asking for postponement of loan repayment. It is also a good idea to ask for legal advice from an expert practitioner to ensure that you have all the information about your rights that you need to lead the negotiation process.

Know About Your Repayment Plan

Typically, the repayment plan for a student loan requires the student to repay the loan within 10 years of expire of the grace period. However, even before you start making repayments, you can explore the alternative repayment options that you possess. You are the customer and the lender will have to change the repayment plan if the agreement gives you the right for the same. All that you need to do is ask them.

Forgiveness Plans

Volunteers, medical workers, teachers and public servants can ask for forgiveness of their student loans. This is a legal obligation. Look for these options and see if you are eligible for such loan reductions. These are particularly given to people with medical impairments. The bottom line is that you must look at the options that the legal framework has given you and do not try to cheat the lender.

The steps mentioned above shall give you the most relaxed startup for student loan repayment. However, if you have taken a government loan and you are taking a course in the government or government-aided college, then the amount of money you owe is significantly less. However, if you took loan from a private organization and took several top-up loans, then the amount of money you owe is much more. Therefore, in such a case, loan repayment can be more difficult and you will need to follow the steps and tips mentioned in the following chapters to manage debt effectively.

CHAPTER 4:

LOWERING RATES OF INTEREST

Although, the rates of interest for student loans are significantly lower as compared to other loans, considering the large repayment period, the total payable interest can be rather large. Moreover, repayments are made against the interest and expenses first. It is at the last that the actual amount borrowed is repaid. In order to reduce the interest, you can follow one of the ways and methods mentioned in this chapter.

Reduce the Capital Borrowed As Much As Possible

The amount of interest payable on your loan is directly proportional to the amount of capital that you have borrowed. Therefore, if the capital is large, the interest rate shall also be large. Moreover, if you manage to reduce the borrowed capital amount, you can make significant reductions in the interest paid and consequently, the monthly amount payable for loan repayment.

You can reduce the capital of an existing loan by paying some amount over and above your monthly installment. For instance, if you are expected to pay $100 per month as the loan installment, try to increase this amount to $120 or $150. This will allow you to finish off your loan faster. However, some loans do not offer the facility of pre-payment and even if you pre-pay your capital, the same interest may be applicable. So, read your loan agreement carefully to see if this option is available to you.

Prioritize Loans

It has been observed that most student loans are not just isolated loans, but they also have multiple top-up loans with them. If you have multiple loans running in your name, you must list out all the loans that you have taken and the amounts you owe for each of them. Also, write down the interest amounts that you are paying for each of these loans.

Mind you, we do not mean interest rates here. Calculate the interest amount you are paying for the loan using the payable rate of interest. Now, look at the loan that has the highest interest amount and attempt to pay it out first. In order to make the concept clearer, let us consider the following example: Suppose you have two loans running in your name. For instance, the first loan is A of $100 borrowed at 2% of annual interest and the second loan is B of $90 borrowed at 3% interest.

By the end of 10 years, you will be expected to pay $121.90 for the complete repayment of loan A, which means that you are paying $21.90 as interest for the loan. On the other hand, you will need to pay a total amount of $120.95 against your loan. In other words, for loan B, you have agreed to pay an interest of $30.95. If you look at the interest paid, then even though the capital borrowed for loan A is higher, the interest paid for loan B is higher. Therefore, you must plan to repay loan B before you decide to pay back loan A.

Negotiate Your Loans

A mistake that most people make is that people go for standard loans and do not negotiate the terms with the lender. You can expect to negotiate almost every aspect of the loan including fees, overheads and even the grace period that you have before repayment starts for you. Never take any of the terms for granted. Instead, understand that every little thing in your loan can be customized and negotiated upon. You are the customer and you must take the product only if it suits you. Moreover, the lender will want to disburse the loan to you and if the buffer is present, he or she will certainly make a customization for you.

Consolidate And Refinance Your Loans

If you have multiple loans running in your name, you also have the option of consolidating them into a single loan. This opens new doors of negotiation for you. Since, the lender, if he or she agrees for consolidation, agrees to make a new loan arrangement for you, your lender also agrees to set new terms for your loan. You may ask for lower interest rates and a more flexible repayment process during the negotiation process. In addition, you may also ask for a longer grace period.

All the tips given in this chapter may seem like monstrous tasks and objectives to achieve, but this is certainly not the case. All that you need is some genuine advice from the legal expert, a call to the lender to set the meeting and an initiative to get the process of negotiation and terms settlement started.

CHAPTER 5:

MANAGING YOUR INCOME

There is no rocket science in the concept that if you need to pay your loans in time, you either need to reduce your loan amount and increase the loan repayment period or increase the source of income. The principle is simple: you have borrowed money and the only way you can repay it is by earning money and giving it back to the lender. So, if the negotiation process and re-loaning framework does not work out for you and even if they do, they still leave you wondering on how you will repay your loan, don't lose hope yet.

There are some other options for you to explore as well. However, in order to implement and get the tips mentioned in this chapter to work for you, you will need to make active changes to your lifestyle and bring in an element of discipline in the way you exist. So, if you have the vigor and determination to do all that you can do to manage your finances and debt, here are a few things that you may consider pondering on.

Save Money

You can hope to make repayments and even pay over and above your expected monthly repayment if you have saved that amount for the month after you have made room for your monthly expenses. However, expenses are like a balloon. The more you air it, the bigger it will become. So, the more room you give yourself to spend, the higher you credit bills will become. Therefore, saving and spending within your affordability limits must become your habit.

In student loans, you have an advantage that you are not expected to pay anything as a student. So, while you are still in college or university, you will not need to pay anything. You may use this time to make savings and create a buffer amount for yourself to bank on when the repayment process begins. In a way, this buffer amount equips you to make repayments timely regardless of whether you have managed to get a job or not.

If you get a job, then you may use the buffer capital to reduce the borrowed capital, reducing your monthly installment significantly, or to pay monthly installments in times of financial emergencies. However, if you do not manage to get a job, you may use this buffer capital to make the monthly repayment during while you are making negotiations with the lender or exploring repayment options.

As a student, you can also earn extra cash by working part-time or selling off anything that you no longer need. Open a savings account and put a part of your monthly income in the savings account. No matter what, never look at the savings account as money that is available to you for spending. By the end of your student days, you can expect to have a substantial buffer capital with you to help you sail through with your loan repayment period.

Keep Away From Other Debts

While you have a student loan on you, try to not take any other loans like a car loan or a personal loan until you repay the student loan in full. The more the loan, the higher will be the monthly installment that you will need to pay and the more difficult will the repayment process become. However, the higher access of easy credit in the form of credit cards has made it very difficult for anyone to keep his or her personal debt to a bare minimum.

You can refrain from increasing your debt by paying for your expenses in cash. So, whenever you go grocery shopping or personal shopping, be sure to make cash payment. This keeps you in control of the amount of cash that you have left with you from your monthly expenditure. Also, you must understand that credit cards allow you to make repayments later on, but you will have to pay interest on the amount borrowed, which can be difficult to bear for you keeping in mind your present financial condition. All in all, you just need to learn how to live within your means.

Look For Alternative Income Sources

The more money you make, the more you will be able to spend and the more you will be able to save. So, do not just rely on the pocket money that you are getting from your parents. Be sure to take up a part-time job to add up to your existing income. Whatever money you save for the month, no matter how small or large, be sure to put it in the savings account that you have created for your buffer capital. Realize the importance of having a large buffer capital. If you save more right now, you will be able to spend more later on. However, if you spend more today, you may not be left with anything to spend, later in your life.

Maximize Your Post-Graduation Earnings

If you manage to get a job after graduation, which is your best-case scenario, you must understand that post-graduation jobs or first jobs usually offer low salaries. Moreover, your earning may also be inconsistent during this period. Therefore, try to run your part-time job along with your main job. This will keep your finances stable and savings consistent. Although, you may feel as if you are working all the time, the effort will be worth all the trouble if you look at the benefits that this time of hard work can yield for you at a later time.

Invest On Skill Development For Increasing Professional Value

Do not just bank on your graduation degree. Your graduation degree may help you get a job, but you can get a better paying job if you invest some of your post-graduation time in skill development and increasing your professional value. For instance, if you have graduated in information technology, you must look at the job market to analyze the skill set that most high-paying job in the IT market requires. Instead of diving into the sea as a novice, take a dive when you are best prepared to face the challenges of the job and get the returns that you deserve.

Manage Your Life

Discipline and persistence are the essentials if you are hoping to make considerable savings in your student or post-graduation life. You can expect to make substantial savings only if you comprehend the difference between what you need and what you want. Keeping in mind the loans that you have on your shoulders, spending on luxuries is something that you cannot really afford.

Also, try to invest the money that you have with you and refrain from taking any new loans. For instance, if you need to buy a car, choose a used one instead of a new one. Besides this, instead of eating out all the time, start cooking your meals at home. These steps may seem like ones that will save you small amounts of money, but realize that in the financial surroundings that you are thriving in, every single penny literally counts.

CHAPTER 6:

DON'T PANIC AND KEEP YOUR COOL

In times of crisis, most people tend to lose their cool and make mistakes that land them up in bigger trouble. Student loans are given out to students and at such a young age, they cannot be expected to show the same level of wisdom and awareness that businessmen and professionals with loans exhibit. However, if you just keep your head cool, you can actually dodge a majority of the issues that people with student loans face.

Set Realistic Goals

Setting realistic and tangible goals is the key to getting it right as far as student loans are concerned. Therefore, when the time for repayment has come, or even before that, be sure to take down all the things you need to do, on a piece of paper. This will keep your thoughts focused and chances are that you will not skip anything important.

Get Your Calculations Right

When you have your goals listed, list down all the details of your income and expenses. Let us them each of them up, one at a time. The first thing that you need to focus on is total income. You must list down all the sources of your income along with the income they are expected to generate on a monthly basis. It is understandable that you may have some temporary sources of income as well. So, you must list them down and list them down.

Star-mark them to ensure that you don't count them as assured income at any time of your life yet you don't miss out on the probable income that they may generate. However, while counting the total income, do not consider them, as they are not assured income sources. Also, do not count in the income your family may contribute because you may or may not be able to get this money and you cannot depend on it completely.

The other side of the coin is your expenses. You need to list them down explicitly citing the amount of your monthly income that they will consume. Be sure to list down every little thing that you can remember even if it is something really small. This list will help you significantly in cutting down your expenses and bringing them to a bare minimum.

However, be sure to cut down only the luxuries. You cannot live without the basic necessities like food, house, water and clothing. Moreover, a little leverage must be allowed as too much constrain may leave you frustrated. You will need to make two lists for expenses – the expenses that exist and the revised expenses that you hope you live by in the following months and years.

If the difference between the income and expenses is equal to or more than your monthly installments for loans, then you are in good shape. However, if this value is lesser than what you need, then you may have to invest some time on contemplation. You will either need to reduce your expenses and if that is not possible, then you will need to work out ways that can reduce your loan repayment amount or increase the grace period so you have more time to accumulate savings and find ways to increase your income.

If you go through the previous chapter carefully and go back to them every now and then when you feel lost in your forays of finance and loans management, you will certainly be able to get yourself into a position where you will be able to manage your student loan and all the top-up loans you have effectively and efficiently.

Look At The Big Picture

Having short-term goals like curbing expenses are some great ways to get your financial condition in shape, but all this while never make the mistake of losing view of the big picture and why you are taking all these steps. All the small steps shall combine together and align themselves in such a manner that they cumulatively contribute to the main goal – getting rid of the loans and managing debt. So, be sure to assess and evaluate the time you need to get rid of the loan in full. It will also keep you motivated in the sense that you will know the time for which you need to restrict your luxuries and expenses before you can let yourself lose and get the car you have been eyeing for some time.

Keep Stress At Bay

Shorter loan periods are not always the solution to debt issues. In fact, if you set the loan period too short, you may stress yourself excessively. In fact, instead of hoping to save money, you may end up in the hospital getting treated for anxiety and stress, spending your hard earned and saved money on something that could have been avoided. So, keep your stress at a bare minimum and look at options that are 'real' options. Don't let frustration and stress creep into your system and ruin your health.

Win a Brand-New 6.6 inch Kindle Fire HD

Open to residents in the U.S., Australia, Canada, England, Europe and India

As part of the launch of Our New Bull City publishing Series,

I'm giving away a brand-new Kindle Fire HD this month. Somebody reading this post will win. The contest is only open to fans and readers who are on my opt-in list.

Here's the deal. Any Customer that downloads one of our books ,writes a nice testimonial, AND places the review on Amazon, you will then be entered into raffle to win a 6.6 inch Kindle Fire HD. The odds of you winning are better than the lottery. I'm thinking only twenty people will actually post a review by the end of the month. If that holds true, you would have a one in twenty chance of winning. That's great odds.

I will take all of the testimonials from Amazon, posted from the 5th, through the 30th of the month, put them in a jar, and randomly pull out a winner. The winner will be announced on the 1st of every month, in an email like this one. The brand-new Kindle Fire will be shipped to your door, whether you live in the U.S., Canada, Australia, England, Europe, or India. Again, all you have to do is purchase one of our Books between now and the 30th and place a review on Amazon by that time.

Why am I giving away a free Kindle Fire? Many reviews of a book help readers to discover new books, and everyone loves to find fresh authors previously unknown to them. Many four and five star reviews will help to validate that our book.

If you're willing to help me and want to win a 6.6 inch Kindle Fire HD, Simply post your Honest review and email me a link of your review to **info@bullcitypublishing.com** with Kindle Raffle in the Subject line

Screw Student Loans

Check Out My Other Books

Below you'll find some of my other popular books that are popular on Amazon and Kindle as well. Simply click on the links below to check them out.

http://www.amazon.com/How-Start-Successful-Hair-Salon-ebook/dp/B00ED8F7EO

http://www.amazon.com/Opening-Boutique-Guide-Clothing-Starting-ebook/dp/B00EOAVAN8

http://www.amazon.com/Becoming-coupon-Warrior-Extreme-couponing-ebook/dp/B00LO8KCBY

http://www.amazon.com/Online-Marketing-Real-Estate-Professionals-ebook/dp/B00EF5DTH2

http://www.amazon.com/How-Read-Body-Language-101-ebook/dp/B00HBUA35E

http://www.amazon.com/Clothing-Line-Start-Guide-Successful-ebook/dp/B00EEWE0PQ

http://www.amazon.com/How-Start-Rap-Record-Label-ebook/dp/B00EE6RAOA

http://www.amazon.com/Hip-Hop-Rhyming-Dictionary-Extensive-ebook/dp/B00FF8SDZ6

http://www.amazon.com/Start-Restaurant-Without-Losing-Shirtebook/dp/B00EETB6Y2

http://www.amazon.com/Play-Piano-Fast-Yourself-Playing-ebook/dp/B00LUQ1SKO

http://www.amazon.com/Fashion-Show-Secrets-guide-fashion-ebook/dp/B00LUPNPTW

Thank You for Your Purchase!!!!!

Thank you again for Ordering this book!

I hope this book was able to provide you with the Information that you were searching for. Lastly, if you REALLY enjoyed this book, then I'd like to ask you for a favor, would you be kind enough to leave a review for this book on Amazon? It'd be greatly appreciated!

Lastly, Please be sure to connect with us We Would Love to Hear from You

Bull City Publishing Social Media Links:

Blog: http://bullcitypublishing.com/blog/

Facebook Group:
https://www.facebook.com/groups/bullcitypublishing/

Twitter : https://twitter.com/BullCityPub

Instagram: http://instagram.com/bullcitypublishing

Pintrest: https://pintrest.com/bullcitypub

Linkedin: http://www.linkedin.com/companies/5311112

Tumblr: http://bullcitypublishing.tumblr.com

Do you Love Reading? Do you Want a Ton of FREE Kindle Books? Join our Mailing list by Emailing us at freebooks@bullcitypublishing.com

Do you Need Help Writing a Book? Would you like to get published? If So Shoot us an email publish@bullcitypublishing.com   publish@bullcitypublishing.com or Visit http://bullcitypublishing.com/get-published/

Thank you and good luck!

James Moore

Made in the USA
Lexington, KY
20 July 2017